How do Computers See?

A Picture Book Intro to Computer Vision

written and illustrated by Rocco Zhang

This is a work of fiction. Names, characters, places, and incidents are the product of the author's imagination. Any resemblance to actual persons, events, or locales is entirely coincidental.

Copyright © 2022 by Lit House Publishing

All rights reserved. No part of this book may be reproduced or used in any manner without written permission of the copyright owner except for the use of quotations in a book review.

Book design by Rocco Zhang

ISBN 978-1-959128-47-2 (hardback)

www.lithousepublishing.com

This is a computer.

They're great with numbers and love doing math!

Since they don't have eyes, computers can't really SEE the way you can.

They can receive and store images . . .

 . . . and they can display them back to you.

But all they know about a picture is whatever YOU decide to tell it.

Name: mountain-view.png
Date taken: 08/08/2008
Description:
"Two mountains and some clouds during a sunny summer day"

Why? It's because computers can only use numbers, so they can't see pictures like we do.

To them, the pretty landscape looks something like this: (note these numbers are random, and not the actual numbers for this image)

Each square represents a pixel, so this "image" is 8 by 8 pixels. Most images are hundreds of pixels long and wide though!

If we want our computer, not just us, to understand what's in the image, we can use **computer vision.**

The type of computer vision we will learn basically does a bit*** of math using these things called **kernels.**

***a BIG understatement

Technically, kernels are like any other math operation, but they operate on whole images rather than single numbers.

So what do kernels look like? Well . . .

Some kernels are small . . .

. . . while others are tall.

Some are quite wide . . .

. . . and some have long strides.

Some are reversed . . .

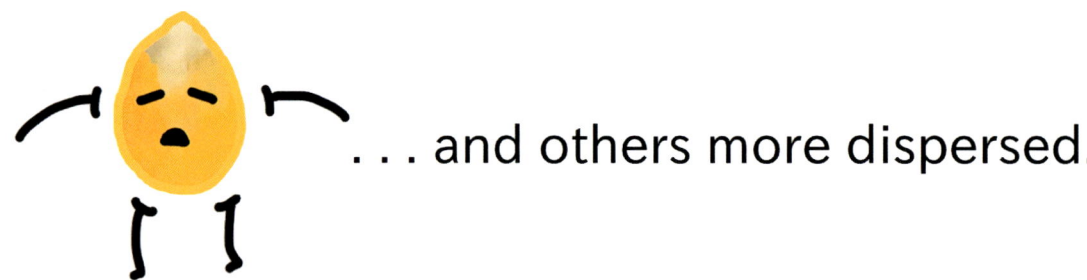 . . . and others more dispersed.

As you can see, they're very diverse!

*Note: There isn't any actual corn in a computer.
Don't open one up and expect to find food!*

When kernels are used on an image, it makes a new image-like thing called a "map". The different kinds of kernels have different ways of doing this.

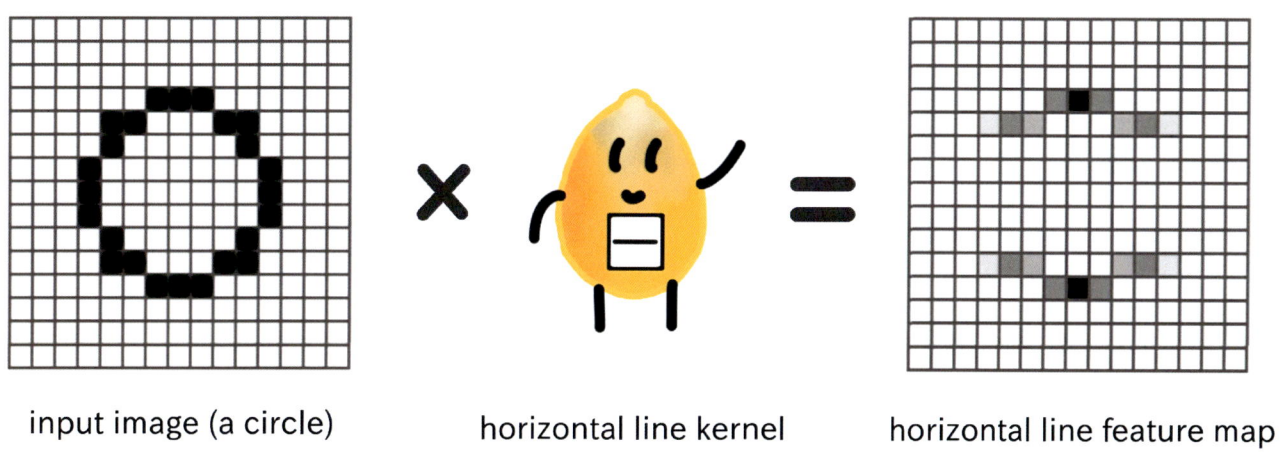

input image (a circle)   horizontal line kernel   horizontal line feature map

These "maps" indicate where and how strong a certain "feature" (such as horizontal lines) is on the input image. That's why these "maps" are called **feature maps.**

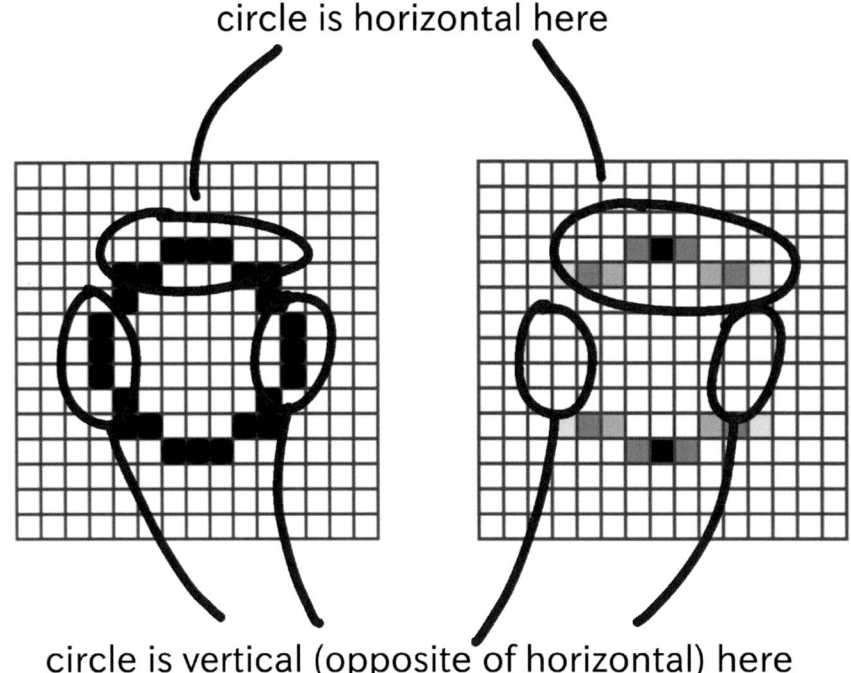

circle is horizontal here

circle is vertical (opposite of horizontal) here

Likes images, feature maps are made up of a bunch of numbers. Here, we use

dark = big number = feature is strong here

light = small number = feature is weak here

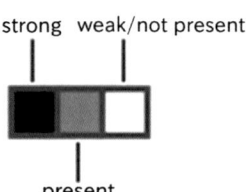

strong   weak/not present

present

Each kernel has its own unique feature, so they each make different feature maps. This process is called **feature extraction**, since the kernels are finding and pulling out features from the image.

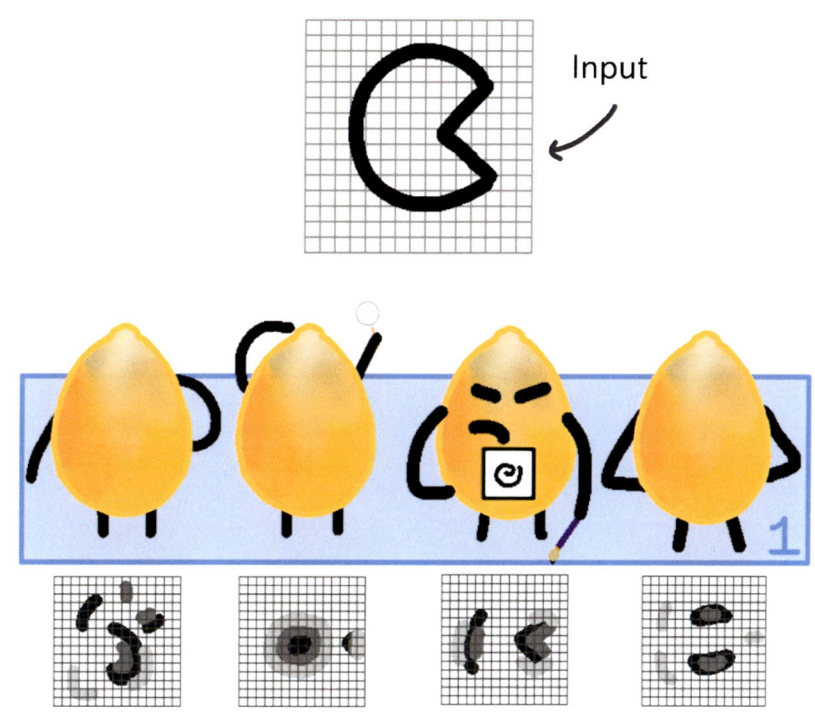

While some features (like vertical/horizontal lines) are obvious to find, many features are complex and hard to understand as humans. This will make some feature maps look like random scribbles.

All kernels that look at the same input image/map make a single **layer**. This first layer will output four feature maps since there are four kernels.

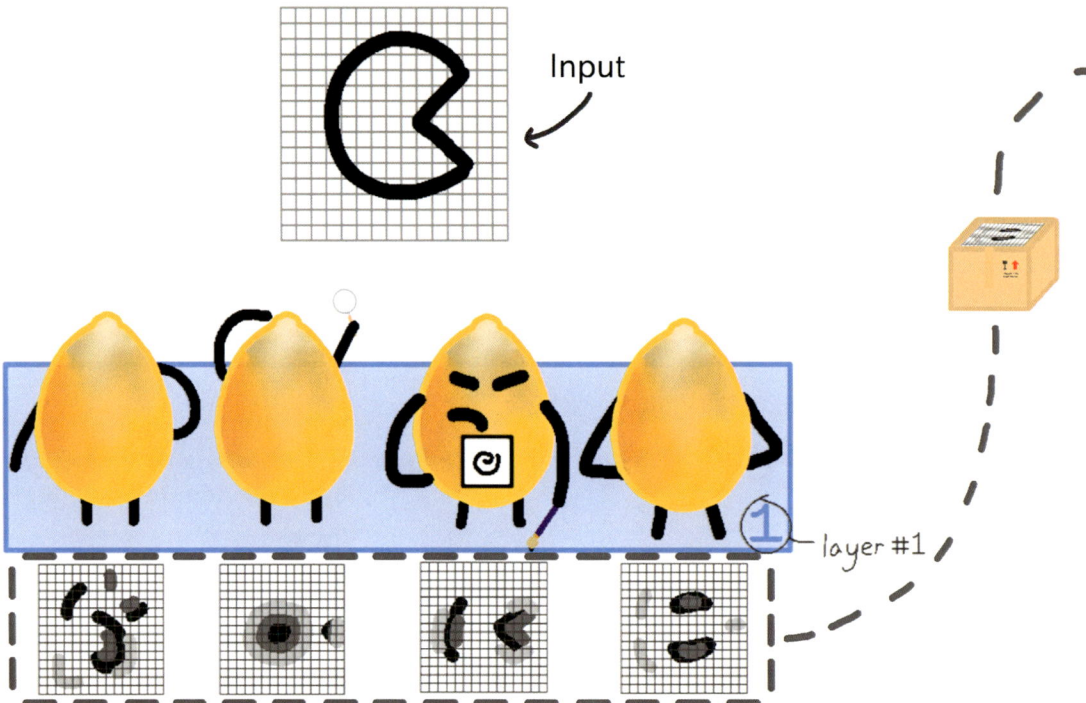

Where does this output go, you ask? Well, to more kernels of course!

Each kernel in the next layer will make a new map for each of the input maps. So for four input maps, all three kernels produce four output maps, or twelve in total.

Wow math!

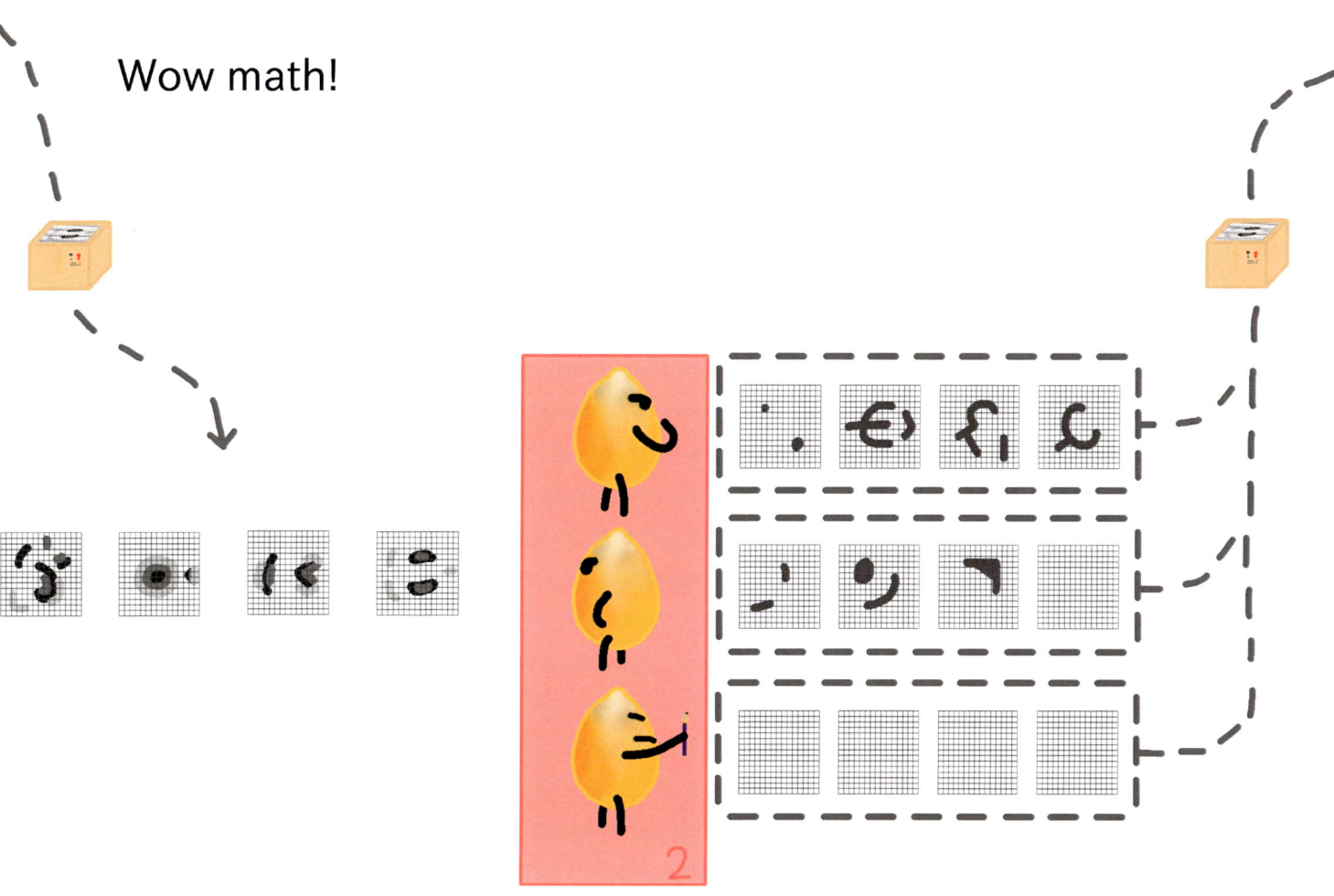

All maps from a particular kernel are compressed together into a single map, representing the feature of that kernel. Here, there are three compressed maps for each of the three kernels in the layer.

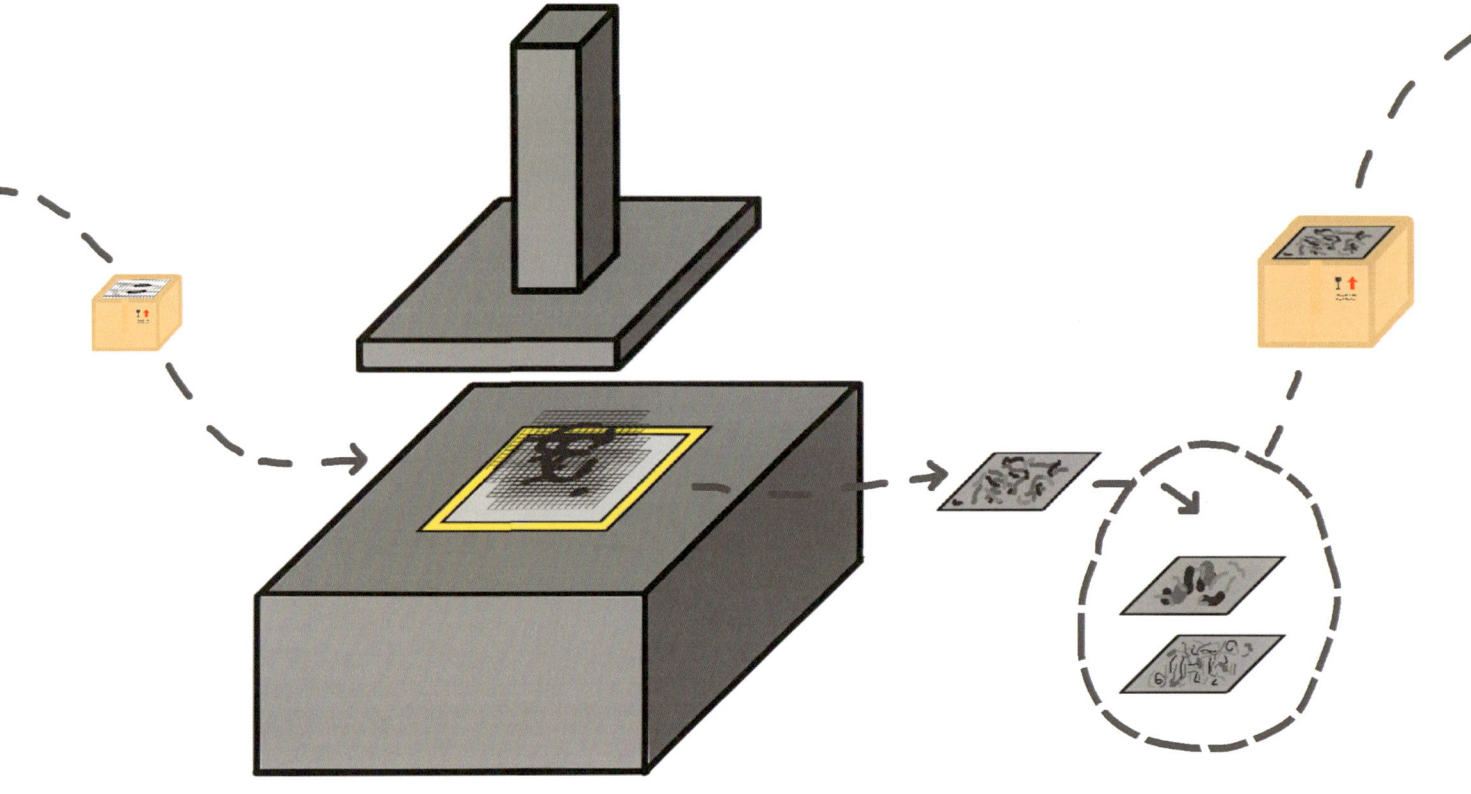

Since these kernels are looking at feature maps rather than the original image, they can see more complex features, like corners and curves instead of lines and dots.

Every following layer repeats these steps, extracting more and more complex features as the number of layers increases. Since there are more complex features than simple ones, later layers have more kernels to make sure all features are accounted for.

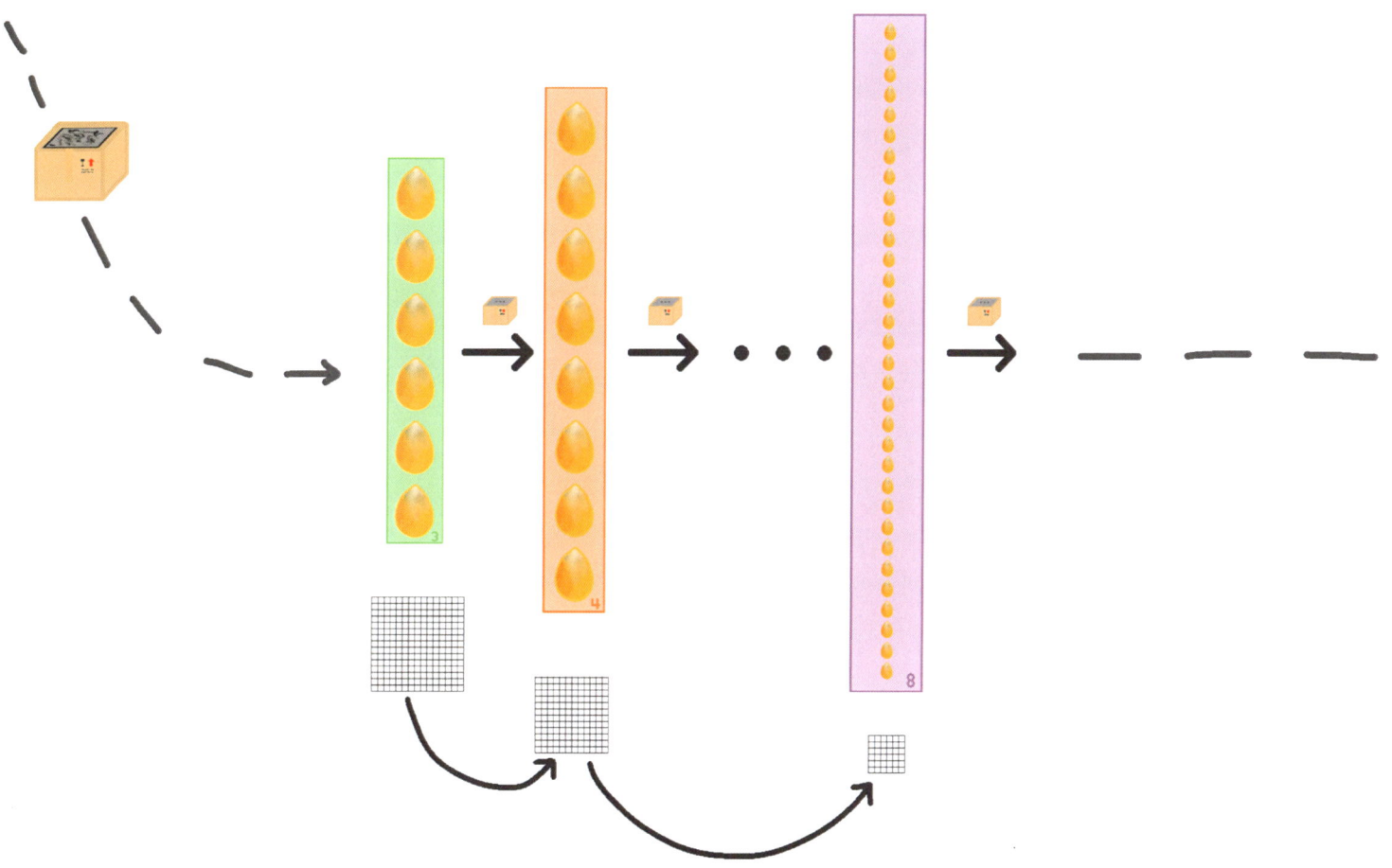

However, more kernels means a more math for the computer, so the maps are shrunk down with each new layer to reduce the math and make things faster.

The very last feature maps are passed to the **fully connected layers**, the brains of our whole operation.

On the inside, they are a dense web of math, and they use this brain-like structure to make a final output on the contents of the image.

→ "Pac-Man"

It's actually possible for the input image to be sent straight to these fully connected layers . . .

. . . but they will have a much harder time understanding it without the feature maps.

The final output indicates what category the image best falls in. These categories are pre-chosen, so the fully connected layers simply point to the one it thinks fits the image the best.

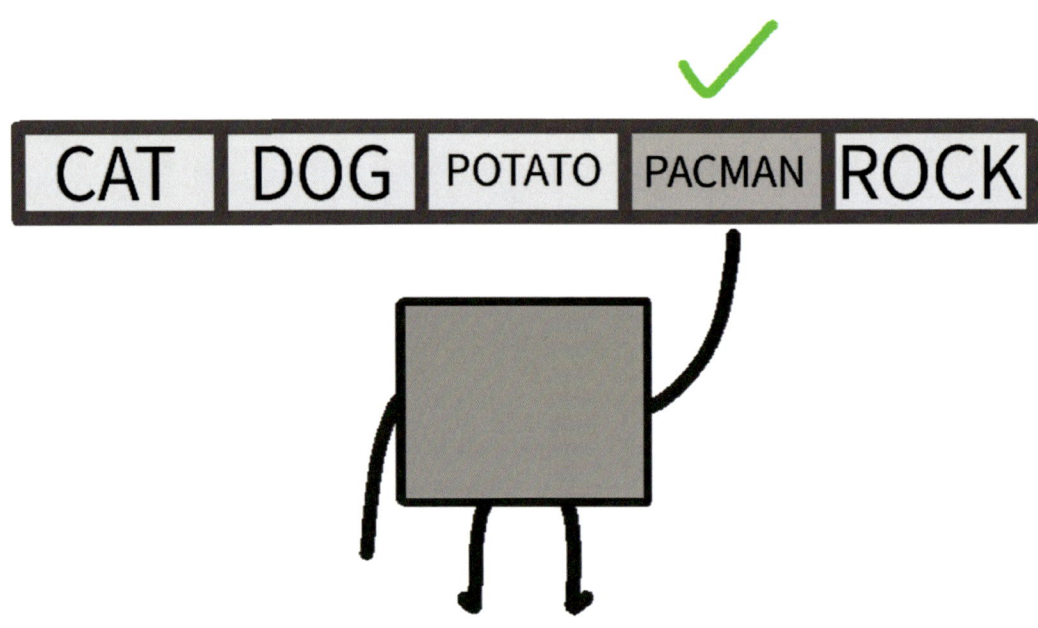

This does mean that it won't know what to do with a picture of something outside the pre-chosen categories, but that's just a limitation of this method of computer vision.

The process for computer vision we learned today is that of a **Convolutional Neural Network** (CNN for short).

Try saying that three times fast!

There are many other wacky ways for computers to "see" aside from this way, and there is a lot more to convolutional neural networks as well. Try exploring them yourself!

Congratulations!

Now you know computer vision. May this knowledge help you in the event of a robot takeover!

www.ingramcontent.com/pod-product-compliance
Lightning Source LLC
Chambersburg PA
CBRC091203010526
44107CB00021B/1234